AN ARBITRARY FORMATION OF UNSPECIFIED VALUE

JENNIFER QUARTARARO

[PANK]BOOKS

Short selections up to three pages may be reproduced. To reproduce more of this book write to PANK at awesome@pankmagazine.com

Cover photograph by Trevor Naud

Cover design by Sasha Ori

Copyright ©2022 Jennifer Quartararo

Library of Congress Cataloging-in-Publication Data

ISBN978-1-948587-29-7

PANK Magazine
PANK Books

To purchase multiple copies or book events, readings and author signings contact awesome@pankmagazine.com

AN ARBITRARY FORMATION OF UNSPECIFIED VALUE

JENNIFER QUARTARARO

For R & our Detroit

WEEK ENDING
10 / 18 / 74

No.

NAME MARY McCALL

MONDAY	IN		
	OUT		
	IN		
	OUT		
TUESDAY	IN		
	OUT		
	IN		
	OUT		
WEDNESDAY	IN		
	OUT		
	IN		
	OUT		
THURSDAY	IN		
	OUT		
	IN		
	OUT		
FRIDAY	IN		
	OUT		
	IN		
	OUT		
SATURDAY	IN		SA SA 10 03
	OUT	6½	SA SA 12 10
	IN		SA SA 12 45
	OUT		SA 4 40
SUNDAY	IN		
	OUT		
	IN		
	OUT		

I am fLesh AND BONES

LATHEM TIME RECORDER CO. Atlanta, Ga. Ptd. in USA

No.			WEEK ENDING 7/19/74	
NAME	Susan McCall			

MONDAY	IN			
	OUT			
	IN			
	OUT			
TUESDAY	IN			
	OUT			
	IN			
	OUT			
WEDNESDAY	IN			
	OUT			
	IN			
	OUT			
THURSDAY	IN			
	OUT			
	IN			
	OUT			
FRIDAY	IN			
	OUT			
	IN			
	OUT			
SATURDAY	IN		SA SA	8 20
	OUT	8	SA SA	12 30
	IN		SA	1 16
	OUT		SA	5 17
SUNDAY	IN			
	OUT			
	IN			
	OUT			

LATHEM TIME RECORDER CO. Atlanta, Ga. Made U.S.A.

			WEEK ENDING	
No.				
NAME		MIKE McCALL		

BLANK

BLANC

MONDAY	IN		M	7 16
	OUT		M	12 03
	IN		M	12 30
	OUT		M	4 20
TUESDAY	IN		TU	7 15
	OUT		TU	12 01
	IN		TU	12 30
	OUT		TU	2 03
WEDNESDAY	IN		W	7 25
	OUT	8½	W	11 58
	IN		W	12 29
	OUT		W	4 16
THURSDAY	IN		TH	7 11
	OUT	8½	TH	12 01
	IN		TH	12 30
	OUT		TH	4 11
FRIDAY	IN		FR	7 24
	OUT	8½	FR	12 02
	IN		FR	12 30
	OUT		FR	4 22
SATURDAY	IN		SA	8 20
	OUT	8	SA	12 59
	IN		SA	1 16
	OUT		SA	5 17
SUNDAY	IN			
	OUT			
	IN			
	OUT			

LATHEM TIME RECORDER CO. Atlanta, Ga. Pld.in USA

I DON'T HAVE ENOUGH oxygen in my blood, I am anemic. There isn't enough oxygen moving through veins and limbs and lungs. This explains why I have dark circles and why I am so exhausted. I walk across dirty floors once overlaid with green shag carpeting and now scraped up, the remaining shag ground down, the texture of fine sawdust.

I am *(fatigued)*.

BELOW THESE CREAKY FLOORBOARDS are hidden swimming pools, deep crevices in the dirt, in the foundations of buildings. There are dry holes in the compacted soil and the river that curves through Dearborn all the way down to Zug Island was once on fire - the flames spewed up from the toxic water and smoke billowed out across I-75. Here the sparks from an acetylene torch ignited oil soaked wooden debris. It took 65 men to control the flames.

I DO NOT KNOW how long Ray and I will be here so we look for rentals; rooms and doors and closets and cupboards we can inhabit for the time being.

THE TERM 'BLIGHT' WAS originally used to describe plant diseases. This includes cucurbit downey mildew, tuber rot and tomato pith necrosis. A blighted area is not capable of sustaining life. A blight is an infection. Blight seeps in at the edges, overtakes from the sides, finds its way in and under sidewalk edges, around slabs of concrete. To be blighted is to be possible of decay, to be infected by a fungus, to watch your stems break down - to see your petals soften and rot.

MEGAN AND I SIT on the porch (a wide cement sidewalk over-looking I-75) of Salt & Cedar Letterpress in the Eastern Market neighborhood and sip French white wine in this most American city, the Motor City, where in 1959 Berry Gordy founded Motown Records using an $800 loan from his family. It took Berry a year to repay his family, and they charged him 6% interest. Today we sip French wine on Riopelle Street, adjacent to America's largest and oldest open-air market, and in between two working meat lockers. We sip white wine while plastic bags spill chicken juice on their way to the imposing green dumpster. We snack on rice crackers and across the street a six year old boy spits out his gum. Somewhere not far away on Gratiot a car is broken into. We sip too much wine and I smoke three cigarettes and tell her I'll be back to help again tomorrow.

ʟ

NEW RESEARCH SHOWS THAT the earth's electromagnetic sur-
face has many impressive benefits for the human body, which is
itself highly conductive. We are 55 - 60% water, made of miner-
als like potassium, hydrogen and magnesium, and so if we walk
across the earth with bare hands and/or feet, we can ease or even
eliminate issues of chronic inflammation. This practice is called,
'earthing'. I could walk through the Michigan Urban Farm Initia-
tive on Brush Street, but avoid the styrofoam that's gathered on the
sidewalk of Oakland Avenue - we are all in reference to ground.

MAXINE POWELL WAS HEAD of artist development for Motown, which meant she taught the artists how to present themselves in public. She saw it as a way to further her race, a way to make African Americans outstanding. For Powell, class and style would be accepted whether the artists ended up at the White House or Buckingham Palace. She taught all of the artists how to glide when they walk. She taught Marvin Gaye how to sing with his eyes open. She taught Florence and Mary and Diana that certain colors make you glow.

A WEDNESDAY MORNING AND I'm off for a run, down the green porch steps to the sidewalk, making a left onto Massachusetts Street towards Oakland. I pass three houses before the neighbor rolls down her passenger window to tell me, "Be careful honey." "O.k." "No, really, there are stray dogs that wander around this neighborhood!" "Is Brush any safer?" "No." "Oh, o.k." There isn't a safer route. There isn't a safe way to go for a morning run. Some Wednesday mornings I don't know what to do with myself.

"YOU ALRIGHT?" BULL ASKS me while I sip red wine on the front porch of Salt & Cedar and watch the cars along I-75 just beyond the chain link fence. After Bull goes back into the meat locker to continue his 10 hour shift Megan asks if I've noticed that people don't ask 'how you doing?', but rather 'you alright?'. It's possible their water could have been turned off or their house could have been foreclosed. Homicides were up 2.3% in 2016. 114 of those were due to arguments, though the nature of those arguments remains unclear. Nonfatal shootings were down in 2016, along with carjackings but someone could have smashed into them on I-94, and with vehicle thefts rising their car could have been stolen. Megan and I set our empty glasses down on the sidewalk and I feel the tips of the dried out potted lavender.

ARBORISTS RECOMMEND REMOVING A tree only for certain reasons, such as when a tree is dead or dying, is planted too close to a power line, is overcrowded or blocks a view. Except for the first formed roots that respond positively to gravity, most roots do not grow toward anything or in any particular direction.

I WALK AWAY FROM Ray mid-arguments to prove my point. If I step away from him, if I am willing to walk into the unknown at any given moment, he might begin to understand how unpredictable I am. I walk away from him mid-arguments because in slow and obtuse ways I want to prepare him for the day that I might leave. I don't want him to say, "I never saw it coming," but rather, "Yes, she has always been walking away from me."

1200 FEET BELOW DETROIT is a salt mine, left there from a dried up ocean that filled the land 400 million years ago, a time period in which elephant sharks swam the waters. The salt deposit lay untouched, covered by dirt and stone until 1895. This mine is the source for all of the salt that is dropped along Detroit's highways in the winter months - this is the salt that gnaws at the paint of the cars.

FOR THE FIRST TIME in 75 years a beaver was spotted upstream by a man in a broken hat. The beaver regularly swims to Belle Isle in search of more bark for food.

THE TREE CANOPY OF Detroit hasn't recovered from a blighting of Dutch Elm Disease in the 1960s and 70s. The disease is caused by a member of the sac fungi and is spread by the elm bark beetle. It is believed to have originated in Asia, though it has since spread to America, Europe and New Zealand. The disease was identified by Dutch phytopathologists, Bea Schwartz and Christine Buisman. It is not specific to the Dutch Elm hybrid.

I WALK TO THE Rite Aid on Woodward Ave. in a light snow for almond milk. It is freezing out. The wind is sharp and intense. Flurries float down from a place I can't decipher. Patches of blue sky peek out overhead, so how are there snowflakes? I can't figure out where they're coming from, but they're large and fluffy and the texture of dust. Like the dust that settles after a fire. Like charred remains. I overhear the woman in front of me make note of the shelf behind the registers. "I just love those giant stuffed teddy bears."

DISUSED FACTORIES ARE CALLED brownfield because of the residue of decades of industrial waste left behind. The brownfield is difficult to redevelop due to the costly nature of removing all possible toxins that have leached into the soil and groundwater, but in the fall of 2018 the city received a $205,00 grant to help with cleanup along a stretch of Jefferson Ave. The former gas station, car repair shop, and bookbinder will eventually be home to 213 apartments and 42,000 sq. ft. of commercial space.

ON MY BIRTHDAY, 28 years before I'm born, Dwight Eisenhower signed the Federal-Aid Highway Act of 1956. The bill created a 41,000 mile "National System of Interstate and Defense Highways" that would - according to Eisenhower - eliminate unsafe roads, inefficient routes, traffic jams and other things that got in the way of "speedy, safe, transcontinental travel." The 1956 law declared that the construction of an elaborate expressway system was "essential to the national interest." On my 32nd birthday, 60 years after the fate of Detroit's highways was decided, I play tennis on the cracked courts at Belle Isle. I bike the nine miles there from Highland Park.

IT IS POSSIBLE THAT in a few years Fourth Street, where Ray and I live, will not exist. The debate about when and how far to extend I-94 has gone on for decades. Commuters note how clogged the highway becomes around this area - the narrow lanes marked with sinkholes and hummocks. The expansion could also remove United Sound Systems, the recording studio where "I Heard it Through The Grapevine" was recorded. At one time the studio was nearly as influential as Motown Records, whose museum recently saw a $50 million expansion. I watch the glowing red and white lights of the SUVs and the pick-up trucks and the mid-size sedans at rush hour from the neighboring, defunct Third Street overpass, and the scene reminds me of the tunnels that ants make - deep, complex networks - except that our networks will collapse one day - these freeways will break us apart in time.

IN THE 1920S URBAN renewal advocates used the term 'blight' as a rhetorical device, which enabled them to reorganize property ownership by declaring certain real estate "dangerous to the future of the city". Blight was elevated into a disease that could destroy the city, on par with tuberculosis and typhoid fever. Renewal advocates broadened the application of the public use clause, and in turn blighted properties became less worthy of the full bundle of rights that governed private property. In a ruling in 1923 the Supreme Court stated that it was, "not essential that the entire community, nor even any considerable portion, should directly enjoy or participate in order to constitute a public use." It was irrelevant how many citizens used the 1,300 churches, homes, stores, and hospitals that were seized in the Poletown neighborhood to make way for the GM Detroit-Hamtramck Assembly factory in the 1980s.

THE BOW ANCHOR OF the SS Edmund Fitzgerald winds up in the Detroit River. The entire crew of 29 died in 1975 when the ship sank after getting caught in a storm with hurricane force winds and 35 ft. high waves. A few different theories circulate about how the ship sank; waves could have engulfed the ship which pushed the bow underwater, causing it to hit ground and break into two pieces. Another theory suggests a series of rogue waves ('three sisters' is the term for three large waves in Lake Superior) may have swamped the ship. A distinctive characteristic of rogue waves is their appearance from nowhere and their quick disappearance. No distress signals were sent out before her sinking, just a message from the captain, "We are holding our own."

I GLIDE AROUND POTHOLES on my bike with the rusted chain and the dented front fender. I feel the blank slates of the pages. I hold paper between hands, between fingers - soft, velvety paper. Some mornings I stop to marvel at the Detroit Institute of Art, its smooth Vermont Danby marble walls. Marble is either made into crushed stone or dimension stone and the crushed stone is used as an aggregate in highways/railroad beds/building foundations/other types of construction, which means the highways are actually marble. That means we are driving along marble- paved roadways. Isn't that romantic? Everyday people tear up pieces of marble.

I WORRY A DEEP Malbec might spill on my sweater. I buy oatmeal colored sweaters because supposedly they flatter my complexion and eye color but then I worry about actually wearing them out because if I wear them, soon they will show signs of wear. It's a vicious, unstoppable cycle. Then there is the wine, there is the wine that I imagine will spill from any number of sources - from the friend sitting next to me at the movie theater, because it is dark and she has already eaten a THC edible on our drive from Detroit to Windsor and now we are watching Yugoslavian structuralist films and so isn't it inevitable that she will lean forward in her chair and the cabernet in her plastic cup will find its way onto my oatmeal-colored sweater?

THE CONCEPT OF 'BLIGHT' worked to alarm citizens, kept them on guard of potential catastrophes in their cities, while the legal power enacted by the federal government now afforded blight the ability to remove any and all neighborhoods or houses deemed unsightly, a vague and subjective set of standards used to systematize classist, racist ideologies, and all tucked away under the guise of legalese jargon. Did anyone ask who the cities were being made safer for?

THE JUICE JOINT OPENS at the back of Marcus Market in Midtown and the counter is next to a display of windshield wiper fluid and motor oil. I point this oddity out one day to the owner and she doesn't laugh with me. I decide not to ask whether she knows that during prohibition a 'juice joint' was slang for an establishment that would sell alcohol illegaly. I don't imagine she would see the humor in that either. The smoothies are too sweet, most combining agave syrup and dates, so I have to ask for custom blends with loads of ginger.

I AM TOLD THERE is iron in red meat but I can't imagine biting into the flesh. They tell me the caffeine blocks the absorption of iron, which I desperately need but I can't picture biting into the flesh and would much rather a chunk of dirt. There are chicken bits at the bottom of the sink that never drain away.

WE CAREEN DOWN 94-W in the backseat of Matt's van during a blizzard, with only metal between us and the wintery elements outside - molded steel that will crush and tear apart should we slide into another car, an aluminum guard rail or a cement wall. The metal is unforgiving and all I want is to feel the sun on my face but there's a blizzard outside and it's nighttime, so we continue to drive to the bowling alley in the snowstorm. I don't have a working seat belt, and I make sure the door is locked again and again and again. I unlock the door so I can lock it. How much snow can we take? Inside the bowling alley I throw 10 pound balls against lane dividers and drink White Russians. A pin gets wedged on the side of the lane, we have to have Steve come dislodge it for me.

OVERQUALIFIED BLACK AUTO WORKERS breathed in ethyl acetate, formaldehyde and methylene chloride in the early 1900s, and thus became more susceptible to asthma as they worked the menial, dangerous jobs at the Ford assembly plants. Red paint contained the highest concentrations of lead. The workers carried molten steel (which has a melting point of 2500 degrees* F) in frantic shuffles - hectic movements of bodies in the foundry that only became more chaotic as production demand increased. The steaming cauldrons could singe and burn and maim. On February 1, 1999 a gas leak in boiler 6 causes a massive explosion at the The River Rouge Complex and kills 6 workers. Flames shoot up into the air and the February that follows is the warmest on record for Detroit.

ACCORDING TO 1930'S URBAN renewal expert Mabel Walker, 'slums'- a term used with, and in exchange for blight - are "a district that has an excess of buildings that either because of dilapidation, obsolescence, overcrowding, poor arrangement or design, lack of ventilation, light or sanitary facilities, or a combination of these factors, are detrimental to the safety, health, morals and comfort of the inhabitants thereof." It is unclear what experts such as Walker thought about the demolition of Paradise Valley - a vibrant black neighborhood in Detroit that would have solidified the city's status as a jazz hub, on par with New Orleans and NYC - in order to make room for a highway. A diminuative green placard marking the historic neighborhood sits in the shadow of the parking garage to Comerica Park, and the grass it sits on is trimmed regularly.

RAY AND I GO for runs around the North End in the mornings, wave to the three old men down the block that sip coffee and chat on their porch. I race him down Brush Street. I sprint between lamp posts and try not to collapse between others. I wonder who used to live in the robin's egg brick house with the wrap-around porch, and if the house is for sale and how much work it might take to repair - will it still be standing in two years? Where will we be in two years? Today we make breakfast together, I chop the kale and grate the zucchini and slice the peaches while Ray pulls fresh basil from the pot on the front porch. Some days I fry the eggs, others I make omelets, and somehow we are always running low on avocados.

A 300 POUND BRONZE statue is recovered from the Detroit river. The figure was part of the Grosse Pointe War Memorial and was stolen from her place overlooking a reflecting pool in 2001. It was designed by Edward McCartan, an American sculptor who received his training in Paris. She is in excellent shape thanks to having ended up in freshwater. There was no salt to strip her sheen.

RAY AND I SPEND our afternoons and evenings for five straight days in the summer of 2015 at the Number House of the Heidelberg Project while we install our show. On a muggy Thursday afternoon in early August, the sky greys and blackens and rain pours down in heavy sheets for twenty minutes. The Number House is boiling, so we open the back door to let more air flow in while a plastic desk fan rotates in the corner of the front room. Despite The Heidelberg Project bringing hundreds of international tourists each year, beyond the perimeter of the project the neighborhood is still considered one of the roughest in the city. As we head out for the day, I smile at the neighbor who sits on her porch every night but who has yet to ever smile back. The sign propped on her lawn notes, "Please don't stare. People live here." I smile anyways because what else is there to do? Several hours later we hop on our bikes and ride through the city as the sun sets. We don't wear helmets and the desolate streets feel post-apocalyptic, survivors of a catastrophe we weren't here to witness. We float along empty roads, avoiding the glass shards.

THE TREE CANOPY OF Detroit hasn't recovered from a blighting of Dutch Elm Disease in the 1960's but a sign marking the entrance to Highland Park, 'The City of Trees', remains intact on Brush Street. The asphalt will break sooner without trees to help absorb the heat. Detroit is the 4th largest Midwestern city so does that mean it has the 4th most concrete? There's no sea breeze in the Midwest and the roads in Detroit buckle and crack under the weight of the elements. There's only so much they can withstand. We all have our limits, we all crack without a sea breeze.

I'M WASHING WINE GLASSES as fast as I can, squishing silk-worms, mealworms and crickets down the drain. The silk worms are caught, they're plugging up the large industrial sink. Tonight is the entomology dinner at Salt & Cedar. It is said that in twenty years we'll all be eating bugs, soon to be the only sustainable source of protein for a population of 8 billion. In time no one will eat steak. We need to wash 20 wine glasses in the next five minutes, we need 30 clean bowls, 30 soufflé cups. I grab from the pile to my right, dip the thin white bowl into the sink, and use the sponge to remove half of a mealworm, an entire silk work, tentacles and sprawled legs and arms. It's only May 26th but the heat is stifling. A thick layer of humidity hangs over Eastern Market - the tar and the pavement and the concrete having soaked up the sun all day - the heat now emanating from the narrow alleys. The meat shop workers have all gone home.

THE DOGS IN THE North End are brutish, an extra layer of security for a neighborhood whose streetlights are slated for possible removal. Each time I bike along Brush or Oakland or Cameron I hear the snarls of broad, muscled dogs through chain link fences. I hear their deep guttural barks, their jaws snapping shut. I hope their leashes hold. There is one pit bull who smells me coming the second I turn my bike onto Oakland Ave. where he runs from behind the dilapidated house, past the picnic table, the sickly maple tree, and I can see his teeth through the wooden slats of the fence. The dog moves with such force that I imagine it is only a matter of days before he pushes through those wooden slats, before he pulls the metal leash free, before he is biting into my thigh, a trail of blood left behind me.

THE MISSION OF THE Detroit Blight Removal Task Force states that they aim to, "develop a straightforward and detailed implementation plan to remove ever 'blighted' residential structure, commercial structure and public building, and clear away every blighted vacant lot in Detroit using an environmentally - conscious approach." The Task Force plans to focus on removal and mechanical demolition of blighted structures. A three person crew can typically remove a structure within three hours. The demolished houses begin to release lead-contaminated dust through the city. The dust can drift through the open windows of the old homes without air conditioning on those hot summer nights when you are trying to get a cross breeze going between the kitchen and the living room.

ACCORDING TO MAXINE POWELL, in time The Supremes want to do more than glow, they want to glitter. The fabrics they wear shift from chiffon and velvet, to skin tight sequin gowns with elaborate feather embellishments and long satin gloves. Part of what sets The Supremes apart from other female groups of their time is that they embrace their femininity, as opposed to trying to emulate the more masculine characteristics of the male groups at Motown. Their signature shade of lipstick is a fiery coral.

IN 1948 THE RIVER Rouge was so fouled by oil sludge and industrial chemicals that tens of thousands of oil-soaked water fowl died. Furious sportsmen loaded them in pickup trucks and drove them to Lansing, where they dumped them on the Capitol lawn in protest. How hard was it to scrub the oil from the beds of those trucks? How long did the smell of dead ducks linger on the lawn?

DETROIT MAKES NATIONAL HEADLINES in 2014 when 33,000 households have their water shut off thanks to a new 'post-bankruptcy austerity policy'. Ford Field never has its water turned off, despite findings that it owes tens of thousands of dollars in back water bills. The same year Galapagos Art Space uproots from Brooklyn to Highland Park, a city where the lead poisoning rate for children is 1 in 7. They buy a former high school, community college campus, and elementary school. Part of their grand vision is to build a 10,000 square foot lake at the center of the venue. Trees will surround the lake but they have yet to specify what kinds.

RAY WOULD LIKE TO show me Fisher Body Plant 21, a crumbling structure in Milwaukee Junction. The building was recently purchased and Ray fears that soon it will be boarded up - impenetrable. A massive brick wall is gaping open, the spot where car bodies were once produced for Cadillac, Ford, and Studebaker. We step over tens of black trash bags, the debris pouring out. Ray notes a nail sticking up from a piece of wood and we keep walking where after WWII, as the Fisher name carried less and less weight, the company chose to focus on buses, ambulances, and limousines. The stairway is further up on the right. I take the pocket-sized flashlight from Ray's hand and lead the way. The last day of limousine production was April 1, 1984. Ray and I climb narrow metal ladders to higher and higher levels of the rooftop. We keep our hands in each other's pockets in between shots to stay warm, to keep feeling in our fingers so we can keep pressing the button of his digital camera - until we can't move our fingers any longer, until we can no longer feel our toes either. We warm up in the car and consider what else must be remembered before it is a different day, before it is a different year. Before it is a different city. Before we no longer want to keep each other's hands warm.

IN A MOMENT OF driving aggression, a man yells out his window, "Move white bitch!" I almost miss the light at Third Street, I almost forget where I am going. I see the former Nabisco-factory-turned-U Haul facility to my right. Nabisco expanded production to Detroit after the success of their Zu Zu gingersnaps and Anola sugar wafers. When U Haul bought the building the basement was flooded. Were there any remaining boxes of gingersnaps floating, the cardboard soggy? Is the brake pedal left or right? Am I speeding up or slowing down? Am I still in the way?

A 1200 POUND REVOLUTIONARY War-era cannon is pulled from the Detroit River. The cannon was originally forged in England in the mid-1700s. Six cannons have been pulled from the river since 1948 and there may be two more lurking below. On a good day visibility is still so poor that divers make discoveries by running their hands along the silty riverbed.

ON A SATURDAY NIGHT Ray and I sit by a bonfire in Hamtramck. We tear up the NYT Magazine and throw pieces into the flames. Large embers float up into the sky and the cauldron fills with blue-green flames from burning the glossy pages. Hiding in these sheets of paper are cranes and serpents, all it takes is a placement of hand on paper, an alignment of forces. At the base of the cauldron are the shiny black chunks that wouldn't burn entirely, the remaining scraps. What was in those slick pages? What chemical compounds couldn't be broken down by fire? What are these pieces of our world that can't be burned, that won't disintegrate?

WHEN THE OLD MAN two houses down dies, I wonder what will happen to the dog he kept in the backyard, the fierce one that snarled through the sheet metal lined up against the chain link fence. Each day that coarse scraping of ragged nails on metal, again and again attempting to claw their way out - the disappointment in his gravelly howl as he slid back down.

DETROIT IS FRENCH FOR 'straight'. A straight is a channel, a sound, an inlet. A straight is a plight. Detroit is a plight. I pedal it's broken streets looking for wildflowers.

EACH DAY IS MARBLE and slate and bone beginning again - marble and slate and bone disintegrating, until we are not a slate at all, until we're only the dust and the dust is in our fingertips, and on the soles of our shoes, those thick rubber soles and it seeps in and it slips all around the edges - fingernails and eyelashes and earlobes and that soft curve of our lips - and we can't help but glow from the dust of the lives lived before us.

I JUMP INTO THE Detroit River on my birthday - we find a modest channel, a bend in the shallow water at Belle Isle. What am I hoping to expose about this place? I turn 32 in the Detroit River while an overactive pit bull tires himself running in anxious circles through the dirt of the shoreline.

RAY AND I DON'T have a car and that makes it difficult to run errands, makes trips to the grocery store hours long. We walk to the Fast Bus (a new express line as of January 1, 2018), ride 25 minutes while I read James Baldwin and he listens to a podcast, gather our needed supplies, walk back to the bus stop, ride the 25 minutes home (I am holding too much to dig out my book so instead we look out the window and point out murals we've never noticed before to each other) and make space in the few cupboards we have to put away the cereal (Ray loves Special K) and the brown rice and the canned black beans, and the salsa and tortilla chips, and the kale, and the potatoes and the coconut milk (I love making curries). We do our best to supplement groceries at the nearby University Market, but the produce is never as good. The kale wilts and the tomatoes are mealy. It's hard to live in a place where sometimes the best we can do is chop underripe tomatoes to put on top of beans and rice. And on certain drizzly nights in early November the yellow leaves gather on the sidewalk in arrangements that are so pleasing, I wonder if a neighbor placed them there, and the rain filters through the few leaves left on the trees and sounds like a ghostly instrument.

IS IT BLIGHT IF you can't see it? Is it blight if it's in the river?

SALES ASSOCIATES AT THE luxury watch and bike store, Shinola, in Midtown wear denim overcoats so it gives the appearance of blue collar workers of the past. The bikes range in price from $800 - over $2,000 for fully custom models. You can get a leather satchel for $600 or a golden latte (that's a latte with turmeric) for $6. Shinola got its start when a research study was conducted and it was discovered that people were willing to spend $10 on a pen made in the USA and $15 on a pen made in Detroit. The company has capitalized on the fact that some components to its luxury watches and bikes are made within the city, though fine print on billboards in the summer of 2017 made note that other components of their watches were made and/or assembled in Thailand. The type would have been hard to read while zooming down I-94 at 80 mph.

ON FEBRUARY 27TH, 1942 a mob of more than 1,000 venemous white people gathered outside of a new black housing project, the Sojourner Truth Project - which was constructed in a predominantly white neighborhood - with a cross as they vowed to keep out black homeowners by any means necessary. Their bodies seethed in anger as they lit the cross on fire.

LAST EXIT BEFORE CANADA.

THE SIGNS ALONG THE highway scream this over and over again. I careen down I-75, keep speed with the other traffic despite my hesitations. 75 branches off abruptly to 375, but it is a left exit, after which I will need to immediately cut over four lanes to get off at Exit 15 - Jefferson Ave. The flattened raccoon is still in the far right lane from three days ago.

TREES DESTROY AND ARE destroyed by a city. In Detroit their roots back up sewers and tear up sidewalks. They are cut off or cut down to make way for expanding streets and rising buildings. Horses gnaw on them.

TINA KNOWS HOW TO spray down the meat grinder. Tina, brassy blonde hair, rail thin arms, worn face, half a cigarette hanging out of her mouth knows at what angle to hold her arms, how to adjust her body weight, and at which angles to shoot the nozzle. She knows which way will send bits of chicken spewing out into the street. The bits make their way across Riopelle Street in the Eastern Market neighborhood of Detroit, land at the edges of my canvas sneakers. I smoke organic American spirits as Bull wanders over from the meat locker next door with a blue pacifier around his neck. His brand new grandson, Jaelyn, is in the hospital. There's something wrong with his blood sugar. He'll need to be in there longer. Jaelyn dropped the first pacifier they gave him, and when it hit the floor the nurses went to discard it but Bull intervened, Bull said, "I'll take that." And now he wears it around his neck, everyday until Jaelyn comes home. Would I like to come over to the pool sometime? (There aren't any public pools within the Detroit city limits, one must have a car to drive to the suburbs) Bull wipes the sweat from his forehead and says, "He's a beautiful baby boy. Beautiful. I'm going to skim the bugs off the top of the pool tomorrow." Comerica Park turns the sky purple with light pollution while chicken juice spills out of a trash bag.

THE FIRST SUMMER I spend in Detroit, all Ray and I do is talk logistics. There is a laundromat in Hamtramck that lets you dry for free with each load you wash. Should we go this afternoon? Maybe we could borrow the van from his friend? Hopefully the battery won't die. If we're already in Hamtramck we could stop at Al-Haramain, stock up on avocados, olive oil, and bulk curry powder. Does Ray have enough on his EBT card to cover the groceries? Could I buy the ice cream because Ray feels strange buying it with his EBT card, like he shouldn't be indulging in ice cream with money from taxes, so instead I buy the ice cream, use the money from a university research grant.

THE Q-LINE, A LIGHT rail which travels along Woodward Ave., opens on a hot day in June of 2017. Admission is free the first week in an effort to entice citizens to hop on. There is air conditioning and free wifi. Ray and I ride the train back and forth on sweltering days. Despite the fact that Detroit is 142.9 square miles, and goes farther east-west than it does north-south, and despite the fact that bus service is notoriously bad, both infrequent and overcrowded, the city opts to spend $144 million dollars on the Q-Line, whose service will eventually be seven miles from downtown to Ferndale but for now is only two miles.

DOES THE BLOOD IN Eastern Market leave a trace? Does the styrofoam?

I SWIRL SRIRACHA, SPICE soy bean paste, and black rice vinegar together in a bowl while waiting for the tofu to cook at a hot pot dinner party and I learn that a few people don't yet know my last name, despite several months of ending up at the same dinner and birthday parties. "Quartararo, it's Italian. My family is from Sicily." "My grandmother told me Sicilians aren't Italian," says a dinner party guest. While in grad school in the Upper Peninsula of Michigan I meet another girl from Maine but when she learns how far south in the state I grew up she declares that part of Maine is basically New Hampshire. We never discuss the ocean and she reiterates her demarcation to anyone that attempts to point out our similar homestates.

THE STRONG WINDS OF late April blow plastic bags into the cherry blossoms on the trees where they get caught in the branches for days.

I'M INVITED TO A bonfire along the canal. It is imagined that the canals, which border Grosse Pointe in the Jefferson Chalmers neighborhood, were used by rum runners during Prohibition. 75% of all the illegal alcohol in the country during Prohibition crossed over the Detroit River. In the winter, sleds carried the alcohol across the ice. Model T cars lay half sunken in the nearby, iced-over Lake St. Clair. Ashland Street flooded repeatedly in the 30s. Today I step into the blue Jeep Cherokee, a weekend loaner from a friend, fiddle with knobs along the right side of the steering wheel, make sure I understand where the blinkers are and where the windshield wipers are in case there's a downpour. I am terrified of there being a downpour, of not being able to see the edge of the road, of not knowing how close other cars are, of the sound of crunching metal, of sliding off the road, of ending up in a ravine.

"I SAW AN AD for a house the other day that advertised it was walking distance to the highway," a friend tells me. "Who would want a house that's walking distance to the highway?"

60 YEARS AFTER BEING dropped in the Detroit River a 6,000 pound steam anchor is retrieved from the water. The anchor came from the Greater Detroit, a luxury steamship that toured the Great Lakes. The steamship had 625 staterooms with amenities such as hand-carved woodwork and intricate murals. After cutting the anchor on December 12th 1956, just months after the Federal Highway Act was signed, the Greater Detroit was towed to Lake St. Clair and set ablaze. The white linen table cloths, the oak tables and chairs, the paintings and even the silverware had already been auctioned off - but the flames engulfed all 536 ft of the ship and marked a fiery beginning to the reign of the car.

THERE'S AN OVERGROWN LOT on King Street, between Cameron and Oakland Avenue where branches line the back alleyway alongside the styrofoam cups, the greasy candy bar wrappers and the dingy napkins. At the edge of the overgrown lot is an empty building painted bright orange where inside beams hang down while light filters through the holes in the ceiling, illuminating the detritus. Three blocks further north along Oakland Avenue is the site of the former Phelps Cocktail Lounge, where George Clinton and the Parliament-Funkadelic played early shows. The building stands in disrepair and a rusted marquee floats over the sidewalk, wires splayed out over the concrete.

Why are these pants on the floor? Why didn't you start dinner yet? For months I berate Ray with an endless list of irritations waiting to be expunged. I never remember why I get upset but I convince myself that extreme fluctuations in mood and disposition are to be expected considering the drop in temperature these last few days of November and the fact that the sun is lost behind a sky of grey. In Michigan we can count our losses for the day, knowing how much earlier the sun has set down to the minute.

THE ENGLISH SCHOOL OF the Ford Motor Company was established in 1913 and classes were offered to employees for free, though they had to attend before beginning their work shifts. They began by mimicking words such as 'tea kettle' and 'soap', the items being simultaneously held by the instructors. During the graduation ceremony the students wore outfits from their varied native homelands into a giant cauldron, a literal 'melting pot'. After a quick change inside the melting pot, they emerged wearing homogenous suits, felt derby hats and waving American flags.

A MAN IN THE neighborhood calls me gorgeous. He doesn't realize I'm wearing this tank top because its 91 degrees out, with a relative humidity of 61%, which means my sweat isn't evaporating which means it feels even warmer than 91 degrees, and I've been biking these wide, hot streets for six and a half miles now and I hate shorts so I am biking in jeans and Ray would like me to come meet him in Hamtramck but I haven't eaten lunch and I can't think, so when this neighbor - wearing a tank top himself - calls out, "How you doing today gorgeous?", I simply wave back. I'm too warm to be offended.

ON JULY 13TH, 1967 Florence Ballard grows tired of the crowd at The Flamingo Hotel in Vegas harassing her about her weight so she pushes her stomach as far forward as she can, reveals her flesh to the abhorrent crowd and the next day Berry Gordy removes her from the group, warns her that if she tries to take the stage he will have her removed. Ballard only became upset after she noticed the extra set of gowns for her replacement, Cindy Birdsong.

I FALL OFF MY bike on Woodward Ave. today - gather myself up off the pavement, scraped and bruised. I am flesh and bones and all capable of shattering in a moment. My knee is bloody but Ray is hoping to go to an art opening. A little girl in a purple dress sees me crying and asks if I'm o.k. Her dress ripples in the wind of a passing mack truck. "I'm alright."

LAURA AND I BOARD the number 14 bus at Warren and Rosa Parks bound for the Rouge River Park and sit for 45 minutes as the bus inches its way west across Warren Ave. We exit alongside brown grass, a guard rail, and a dirt path lined with jagged rocks and dandelions. "The Rouge River was a great place to dump a body," Laura says as we amble along the grass. It's been a dry summer and Laura comes prepared with a wide-brimmed straw hat, sunscreen, a blanket, plates, napkins, cheese, day-old baguette, almonds, a glass bottle of water, and two glasses. I bring a book and wear black linen pants. Neither of us has thought to bring a map, and Laura feels confident that if we walk north, we'll stumble across the river. Laura has lived in Detroit for five years and has yet to explore this park, which lies so far west that you leave the city and enter Dearborn, then eventually re-enter Detroit. We walk north, see a path that edges along the encroaching forest, and decide to follow it through a thick cover of deciduous trees, green and yellow leaves filtering the afternoon sun. We climb up and over meager pine needle-covered hills, grooves and hollows in the earth. We spot what appears to have been a creek but the creek bed is now a thick layer of clay with cracks, dried out. The wind rattles the glasses in Laura's bag - there is no water here.

CONCRETE IS AN INFERIOR version of ground compared with dirt. It's earthing effects are limited, but it is better than linoleum, it is better than vinyl. On the fourth of July Ray and I nap on a slab of concrete by the riverfront, our own private beach.

"THE BASS IS MAKING asbestos fall from the ceiling," a friend casually notes while we watch bands play inside an old airplane hanger at the Coleman Young Municipal Airport in late fall. We giggle for a long time, our laughs muffled by the blaring electronic noise.

RAY SAYS THE TOMATOES taste fine. Ray thinks they are o.k. This is not what tomatoes are supposed to taste like I tell him. Please don't buy the roma tomatoes from University Market again. They are too depressing for this dead end street.

WHEN AUTO INDUSTRY JOBS move further and further out in the suburbs in the last half of the 20th century it is the most vulnerable employees, the inner city residents who have been frozen out of suburban housing markets, that are the ones who must rely on the most expensive private transportation, cars. This job disparity is called a 'spatial mismatch'. Today there are 51 communities that have opted out of the SMART Bus system, meaning inner city residents lack reliable public transit options to the suburbs.

THERE IS A ZEBRA mussel-encrusted Mercury Capri at the bottom of the Detroit River. It's unclear how long it's sat at the bottom of the river, or how it found its way there, if the driver is o.k. When a bonnethead shark was found in the river, it was barely breathing. It is assumed that the shark was dropped in the water, a pet release or a prank. Its stomach was empty.

I DECIDE TO RING in the New Year alone. A friend hosts a pre-going out party in Southwest and while there I learn many friends are convening in Hamtramck for the countdown. I text Ray at 10:38, "Going to tag along with some people to Bumbos! Be back later." A friend buys a round of fireball shots just before midnight and I start 2019 off filled with warmth, my throat burning.

THE GILDED FAÇADE OF a former opera house-turned-parking garage towers over three scattered cars. The scaffolding of the stage can be seen on the second level, grand and imposing and only left because its removal would compromise the structural integrity of the building. The mezzanine level was initially reserved for black-tie invited guests and had gold foyers and subdued lighting. Now all it takes to roam the mezzanine level is a suggested $5 donation. The theater replaced the garage where Henry Ford built his first automobile, the quadricycle. The birthplace of the automobile, replaced by a movie theater, then reclaimed by the automobile. The day after the theater's closing it was said there was nothing spectacular about the final curtain call, just people shuffling along the grand red carpet to watch a final screening of "The Spy With A Cold Nose".

SOMETIMES DAIRY COWS EAT feed that's been supplemented with powdered limestone and marble. Do they glow from the dust of the marble?

I FIND SCRIPPS STREET. There is a platter of sushi, chilled white wine, and a grill filled with veggie skewers - zucchini and summer squash and red onions. I bum American Spirits when I no longer know how to occupy my hands. The canal is a shade of green I've never seen, like a tropical lagoon, and it connects to the river, and it is wide enough only for a single boat. The backyard sits next to the canal and the bonfire is at the edge of the grass so that as the few boats pass we say hello and the boaters hear us. A man and his young son pass through and I wonder if I should invite them to have some grilled zucchini or if maybe I would like to step into their boat? It's not my party, and it's not my boat so I opt against both and instead watch orange flames illuminate the green canal.

THERE'S NOWHERE TO SWIM but we're flooding. The pools were drained years ago. There's nowhere to slip under water but I'm soaking anyway. Are we drowning? The river swallowed up ships and now the freeways swallow up the cars because there aren't enough pump houses for all of the freeways and there aren't enough generators for when the pump houses lose power and what did Charles Lindbergh's mother do each time her basement flooded on Ashland Street?

"OBSOLESCENCE," WROTE HENRY FORD II in response to critics of plant closings, "is the very hallmark of progress." Is that why all of these street lights are under surveillance for possible removal on Oakland Avenue? Is that why my bike rides home at 11 pm are made in darkness along Brush Street? Is that why there's a plot of land in the Amazon of Brazil with an abandoned town called Fordlandia? The town Ford had grand visions to turn into his own rubber-centric production facility. A town whose sole focus was production. Is that why all of the rubber trees died?

I DREAM OF THE west coast - stepping toes into the Pacific, endless valleys of green ferns, orange trees and lemon groves, the smell of citrus and succulents on early morning jogs, bike rides through lush gardens. Hills and valleys and distant snow-capped mountains. I want to disappear into the side of a mountain, turn a bend in a path and be indistinguishable from the evergreens. Instead I make my way down Brush Street, three lanes wide. I am so visible here, the only woman on a bike for miles.

BOBLO ISLAND, AN AMUSEMENT park home to rides such as The Nightmare, Wild Mouse, and Screamer, was accessible only by boat. This now defunct place makes its way onto t-shirts, and is sold in a shop in Midtown where suburbanites visit on day trips into the city. They note how 'nice' Canfield Street is, how 'nice' it is to see the city coming back. Middle-aged white suburbanites come into this shop and point and exclaim over the Boblo Island t-shirt. It is not discussed by any of these people that for many years the island remained segregated, a space for white people only. No one mentions the fact that the owner of Boblo Island fought for years to keep the island from integrating, that it required civil lawsuits, and that at one point he claimed the Detroit River was exempt from American law though his claim of 'open waters' didn't hold up. None of the people looking for t-shirts of the old Tigers Stadium talk about whether their grandparents or great grandparents made the black people of Detroit feel safe or welcome or whether they were of the many that fought to keep water fountains and swimming pools segregated. Were their great-grandparents in the crowd that stoned Alexander Turner, the first black surgeon on the day he attempted to move his family into the home he bought in a white neighborhood? Did they throw stones or rotten potatoes? Who knows the name Ossian Sweet? When fall comes the Boblo Island t-shirts go on sale, 25% off.

AN OUTBREAK OF TUSSOCK moths attacked the trees of Detroit in the early 1900s, and the city goes so far as to hire children to pull the eggs off. They are paid by the egg.

BLANK MEANS 'COMPLETE' OR 'absolute'. There is nothing complete about Detroit, despite the prevalence with which the city is described as a 'blank slate', beginning in the early 2000s. The word is being used as an adjective, but a more appropriate use of the term would be its use as a verb. To "blank out" a space. To cover, to obscure, to cause to appear blank. To blank out means to defeat without allowing the opposition to score. The word comes from the Old French word, 'blanc', meaning white. Perhaps that is the most appropriate usage of the term, to "white out" Detroit. In the North End the bull dozers continue to decimate homes.

WHEN I AM SAD I listen to songs that make me cry. I play them on repeat at work while I water the air plants and make sure the candles are fully stocked. I could get through eight hour shifts without tears welling up if I didn't listen to "You and I" by Stevie Wonder on repeat. Did God make us love each other?

A MAN APPROACHES ME while I read on the steps of the Detroit Institute of Art. He tells me I should keep reading, it's good to learn and he wishes he'd stayed in school. Across the street his mother used to sweep the floors of the Detroit Public Library at night. He never did finish school though, and now he drinks beer out of a paper bag on the DIA's marble steps. I listen to Eddie talk until my ride pulls up along Woodward Ave, and then I watch Eddie meander across the grass, disappearing behind the side of the marble building.

I WANT TO BUY the pink building at 570 East Grand Boulevard, the empty one amidst the long stretch of nursing homes. This strip of Grand Boulevard was once considered the most prestigious address to reside in the 1910s. The homes were cut up into apartments after WWII, most of which later became group homes. The "East Grand Boulevard Convalescent Home" blares funk music on their patio as I bike by. A group of wheelchairs are gathered together on this crisp June day, while blue-grey clouds float overhead. The neighborhood is cheerful, despite the abundance of vacant homes. I speed up through the yellow light (the streetlights are still in operation here) because I'm late meeting a friend at Sister Pie. I hope for strawberry rhubarb.

WHAT ARE WE LOOKING away from when we want to tear a house down? When we call things blighted? What are we trying to rid ourselves of?

TREES DESTROY AND ARE destroyed by a city. Cities destroy and are destroyed by trees. People destroy and are destroyed by cities.

WHILE RIDING THE NUMBER 23 bus to the Meijer grocery store at Eight Mile, I overhear one man tell another, "Fuck that Q-Line, that's so white people can park their cars and be inconspicuous. A lot of black owned businesses shut down while that was being built, people couldn't get into their stores."

THE FOLLOWING DAY THE automated voice of the Q-Line tells me to 'press blue button for stop' and I turn to Ray and note, "shouldn't that say, 'press *the* blue button'?" Because the train goes along the busiest street in Detroit, it is not uncommon during the first months of service for cars to park on the tracks. This slows the train down indefinitely, while we wait for people to emerge from CVS, picking up their prescriptions. On especially comical days cars break down over the tracks, tow trucks required to pull them away.

WHEN IS A FLOWER complete? When the seeds sprout? When it flowers? When it turns to compost?

IF RAY AND I grow old together, an unlikely scenario, we won't ever be able to show younger family members the first apartment we lived in. Each Monday we continue to sort out our recycling, put the 4/5/6 plastics in separate bag from the 1/2 plastics and then walk the overpass above the Davison highway and bring the sorted items to Recycle Here. Construction has begun on a new bagel shop across the street on Holden.

WHAT'S THE MUSCLE MEMORY of driving? The freeways gutted Hastings Street in Paradise Valley, the once vibrant black neighborhood. Can anyone still hear Sam Cooke or Billie Holiday playing The Paradise Theater? Does anyone still try to turn left onto Hastings Street?

I WALK UP BEAUBIEN on a clear, frigid day in February and hear the sound of two ravenous beasts across the street. I freeze when I realize there is no fence and the dogs are headed straight for me. They run full speed and it is only the sound of a woman screeching from the back of the house that causes them to turn around, inches away from me. I am shaking and the bare sidewalk glitters from the sun shining bright overhead.

ON A DAY WHEN the wind knocks over trash cans in early January, Ray and I solidify our break, and then walk a mile to get breakfast at Honest Johns. It is 12:30 but I would like eggs and toast and an endless cup of coffee. Afterwards, we check out the Black Bottom exhibit at the Detroit Public Library. Wooden posts mark the streets, and archival images wrap around the wooden posts, so it is as though one is actually walking through the neighborhood. I look for Hastings Street, the main hub of Paradise Valley. Most of the photos were taken in 1949, the year my mother was born. I try to find images from her birthday, October 12th.

THERE IS THE HEAT that kills old people and there is the cold that kills old people, both just as brutal.

ON A SECRET SANTA survey at work, the last question is, "Any-thing else we should know?" I write, "I miss the ocean. But I hate ocean scented things." It is an ache. Our tears have salt in them, our sweat has salt in it. Salt is preservation, healing, and in Ethiopia salt was literally money, the bars of amole in use as recently as the 1900s in remote areas. 10 - 12 inches long and 1 ½ inches thick, the bars were also black. On the first day I find a gift in my stocking it is a plastic figurine of an orca whale on a surfboard riding a wave and wearing a straw hat. It is the saddest thing I've ever seen and I cry on my lunch break, taste the salt run down my cheek.

OMINOUS PILES OF GRAVEL and rocks soften and thaw early on a day when a thick haze hangs over Gratiot Ave, blocking out the tops of buildings downtown. Is something being torn down or is something being built? Are the stones being set in pace or are they being torn apart? The piles look like Incan ruins rising out of a Peruvian mist. Still, the styrofoam cups.

IN THE FALL OF 2018 the GM Detroit-Hamtramck Assembly, closes. The factory that pushed out churches and schools is now itself doomed. This is where the "Volt" is assembled, and in press releases about the closing it is never mentioned how many jobs will be lost, instead the change is called a 'restructuring', which in actuality involves laying off almost 900 workers in Hamtramck. It is unclear whether Shinola will choose to take any of these newly unemployed at their high end boutique hotel, set to open in early 2019. It is unclear whether the hotel employees will be required to wear denim overcoats.

THE SUPREMES' SEQUIN GOWNS, designed by Bob Mackie, could have been lined with silk, a breathable, soft, shiny fabric. The chiffon of their earlier dresses would have been slightly rough to the touch, due to the semi-mesh weave that also accounts for its transparent appearance. Silk though, the silk is soft, each pound of raw silk requiring the deaths of 2500 caterpillars. The fabric moves closer and closer to the girls, now fitted against their waists and hips, no longer flowing away. They glitter from all angles.

I BIKE ALONG CASS Ave. with flimsy gloves and lose feeling in my fingertips. I worry I've got frostbite, that I'll never type again.

I ARRIVE AT A friend's birthday party in Corktown and enter the half lit home of her parents, candles placed all over the open surfaces. February 24th brings record breaking winds and it's not until an hour later that I realize the candles are half-ambiance/half-utility, since the power is partially out. The potluck dinner includes, among many other things, five types of cheeses, butternut squash soup, and haloumi and pomegranate salad. The lights stay on in the kitchen and dining room but the second floor bathroom remains unlit.

WHAT ANIMAL JUICE SPRAYED out of the plastic bag that was hoisted into a green dumpster the day these leather boots were made?

I MEET A BOY with the same birthday as me at karaoke night. I don't perform and after talking more I reveal I've always wished I could sing, and not just sing because technically anyone can sing, but I wish I could sing *well*.

"What kind of singer would you be?"
"A Supreme, sequin dress era."

TODAY STEEL GREY CLOUDS spewed in the western sky, but I couldn't tell where from. Last week clouds of charcoal smoke pummeled out of the parking garage by the hospital along John R., the former home to the Gotham Hotel, a prominent hotel owned by black businessman, John White. It was also the workplace for a young Maxine Powell, who was employed as a manicurist there in the 1940s. In 2013 Detroit put seven shuttered firehouses up for sale in an attempt to avoid bankruptcy, but still filed for bankruptcy later that year, the largest municipal bankruptcy in the country to date. I don't hear nearly as many fire trucks as I see clouds of dark smoke.

I AM FLESH AND bones and lines and muscle and fat tissue. I am bruises and varicose veins and fading tooth enamel. There is no way to rebuild tooth enamel. You wear away bone long enough and it can't be replaced. Bone on bone on metal on bone. Slicing and cracking. Pulling and tearing with every single carrot.

RAY'S CHEEK FEELS SO soft that sometimes I take this as a sign we should stay together. Who else's cheek would feel as nice pressed against mine?

MEGAN GETS AN EVICTION notice from her landlords in May of 2017. I spend hours that month at Salt & Cedar, packing up the entirety of the 3,000 square foot press into 21 palette boxes. In go the archival prints, the tea kettles, the bird skeleton she saved because it was too beautiful not to save, the family photographs, and the linens from her mother. When people trickle in throughout the month to say their goodbyes, sometimes Megan directs them to a nook piled high, hands them a box to fill, then offers a chair on the porch. It is better we remember the sound of the cars on 75, the smell of the exhaust from the neighboring meat locker's delivery van, how the green door looks when the glow of the setting sun casts over it. Megan has us place things inside and then take them out of the palette boxes. Some days we spend an hour undoing the previous hour's work. I am careful with the dead bird.

We will rise from the ashes.
We will rise from the ashes.
We will rise from the ashes.

I'M HAVING AN ALLERGIC reaction to something, to what I don't know. My skin is covered in hives and I'm worried Ray and I won't be able to build a life here in Detroit. My skin is hot to the touch, I need to get out of here, so I look up cheap flights to Delhi. Will they flag me at security with these red bumps on my face? Ray is three hours late coming home and I watch the lightning storm from our bedroom window, giant cracks of brilliant blue flying across the darkened sky.

THERE'S A PIECE OF black plastic bag at the top of the stairwell in my building that's been there for a week and every time I walk to my apartment door I think it is a giant cockroach, but it's just the same torn piece of plastic bag. It has become a ritual, the alarm at some unknown intruder in my apartment building, and then the flood of relief that it is only a plastic bag.

THE MOST PROMINENT VISUAL feature on post-WWII homes is the garage. Because Americans want function and style, garages are built in styles as varied as Old English, Colonial, and French. Decades later, the opulent garages connected to abandoned homes have yet to be repurposed as movie theaters or opera houses.

I FIND MORE ACTIVITIES to not invite Ray to, like the co-worker's birthday party in early January where I notice a girl holding a beer and standing alone against the wall, her shoulders slumped forward. I walk up and introduce myself and learn that Amy is studying MMA, and by that she means she is watching a lot of youtube clips of Jackie Chan movies. I can't tell if she is serious or if this is an elaborate joke but we talk at length about the nonexistent tree canopy of Detroit. She knows about the blighting, she knows about the tussock moths.

WHEN PERFORMING FOR THE Queen of England The Supremes opt for high-neck, floor-length, beaded gowns. It was joked that some little old women must have gone blind beading those gowns.

I HAVE A KARAOKE-INDUCED anxiety attack in Highland Park on a frigid night in early March, when a snow squall blankets the grim parking lot of the Powerhouse Gym with a dusting of white. A friend pushes me to sing "Can't Take My Eyes Off of You" - the Lauryn Hill version - as a duet but two lines in she shoves the microphone into my face. I crack, push the microphone away, leave the room and gather my coat. The tears continue to well up hours later.

AN EXILED GLACIOLOGIST ATTEMPTED to design an unsinkable aircraft carrier made out of ice. The ice was reinforced with plastic but the project was never completed. How long did the ice take to melt? Are there water droplets from that ship in the Detroit River?

A PART OF ME instinctively wants to get defensive at Bull's noticing of my red lipstick, but I sense he means well. It's all just part of the banter and he means these things affectionately. They are terms of endearment. This is the same reason why the bus driver calls me 'baby'. And what can I do except smile and take a drag of my cigarette and watch the boxes of chicken pile up in the back of the white delivery van. Me in my red lipstick and that freeway over there. Me in my red lipstick and all those dead carcasses next door.

I WATCH THE TRASH disappear and then reappear at my bus stop through the winter. On unseasonably warm days the snow and ice melt, revealing Korbel bottles, crushed cigarette packs, soda cup lids, crumpled napkins, and glistening BBQ potato chip bags. A few days later it is all covered in a dusting of snow again. The branches of a dead tree are encased during an ice storm in mid-February. It is so beautiful, if also treacherous. I must be careful where I place my feet, I could slip at any moment. I could be taken out on this desolate stretch of Oakland so I keep my shoes and mittens on and avoid seeing how the ice might feel against my exposed skin.

(We are all in reference to ground.)

WILL I LEAVE A trace on this city? What reminders will there be of Ray and I? Am I the flower seed or the styrofoam?

I SPEND MOST OF the winter fixated on the number of empty lipsticks tubes that end up in the ocean every year. (It is around 960,000 tons of cosmetics plastics, of which that number it is hard to determine exactly how many were tubes of Candy Yum-Yum, All Fired Up, or possibly Lady Danger.) The tubes are difficult to recycle, and the lead contained in shades like Power Move - a deep burgundy - contaminates the landfills. The plastic tubes won't break down for 500-700 years while outside our building no one shovels the slushy sidewalk.

POWELL TAUGHT THE SUPREMES the proper way to do the The Shake - the buttocks is tucked under, while you smile and shake to the floor.

DECEMBER 28TH IS TOO warm for Detroit. The sun comes out from behind the clouds in the afternoon and temperatures reach 50 degrees. People note how pleasant it is outside, what a beautiful day it is. I tell a coworker it feels ominous. When I step out of work to walk home there is hail - ice pellets scrape my cheeks and I'm scared that if I step away now it can't be undone. Ray and I wake the next morning to a thin dusting of snow on the windshields of cars along Fourth Street. If I squint hard enough it is always snowing in Michigan.

I CAN'T PICTURE THE flesh there in my mouth. Swallowing down the limbs and extremities of a cow, of a pig, of a chicken - all made smooth and consumable. I can't get past the thought of blood trickling down my throat, crunching on bones, sucking the bones clean of the flesh. I would rather the silkworms, I would rather the dirt.

S/1

No_____ WK. ENDING _____ 19__

NAME Julianne Wash

REG. HRS	RATE	AMT.
O.T. HRS.	RATE	AMT.
SAT. O.T.	RATE	AMT.
COMM.		AMT.
DATE		ADJ.
SOC. SEC.	40	TOTAL WAGES
WITHHOLD	540	160.00
UNION DUES	11	
ADVANCES	20	
INSURANCE		TOTAL DEDUCTIONS
LAUNDRY		
REPAIRS		4311
BONDS		
		NET CHECK
		116.89
		# 4162
		7/11/74
CHECK NO.		

Form 5-14

DESTROY PEOPLE

No.				WEEK ENDING
				6-1-74
NAME	R. Anderson			

MONDAY	IN	8		TU 7 29
	OUT			TU 11 56
	IN			TU 12 24
	OUT			
TUESDAY	IN	9		W 6 35
	OUT			W 11 55
	IN			W 12 28
	OUT			
WEDNESDAY	IN			TH 6 56
	OUT			TH 11 55
	IN			25
	OUT			
THURSDAY	IN			6 47
	OUT			58
	IN			29
	OUT			
FRIDAY	IN			
	OUT			
	IN			
	OUT			
SATURDAY	IN	5		SA 8 47
	OUT			7 00
	IN			
	OUT			
SUNDAY	IN			
	OUT			
	IN			
	OUT			

DESTROYED by CIT S

& ARE

LATHEM TIME RECORDER CO. Atlanta, Ga. Ptd. in USA

				WEEK ENDING
No.				7/12/74
NAME	ROB'+ O. MUNGER			

		IN		≡ 7 27
MONDAY		OUT	7 3/15 p	10 m
			BLANK	Touh 4:30
TUESDAY		IN		≡ 7 15
		OUT		
		IN	BLANC	Lower
		OUT		4 03
WEDNESDAY		IN		≡ 4 04
		OUT		≡ 7 13
		IN	8 1/4	
		OUT		≡ 4 02
THURSDAY		IN		≡ 7 32
		OUT		
		IN	8	
		OUT		≡ 4 01
FRIDAY		IN		≡ 7 23
		OUT		
		IN	8	
		OUT		≡ 4 03
SATURDAY		IN		
		OUT		
		IN		
		OUT		
SUNDAY		IN		
		OUT		
		IN		
		OUT		

LATHEM TIME RECORDER CO. Atlanta, Ga. Ptd.inUSA

No.			WEEK ENDING	
			9/27/74	
NAME OSCAR COLEMAN				

MONDAY	IN			= 8 10
	OUT			= 12 00
	IN			= 12 30
	OUT			= 4 00
TUESDAY	IN			= 7 57
	OUT			= 12 0?
	IN			= 12 31
	OUT			= 4 0?
WEDNESDAY	IN			= 7 28
	OUT			= 12 00
	IN			= 12 28
	OUT			= 9 00
THURSDAY	IN			
	OUT			
	IN			
	OUT			
FRIDAY	IN			
	OUT			
	IN			
	OUT			
SATURDAY	IN			
	OUT			
	IN			
	OUT			
SUNDAY	IN			
	OUT			
	IN			
	OUT			

		WEEK ENDING
No.		7/10/74
NAME	MATT Liparoon	

				OF THE marble	
MONDAY	IN				
	OUT				
	IN				
	OUT				
TUESDAY	IN				
	OUT				
	IN				
	OUT				
WEDNESDAY	IN				
	OUT				
	IN				
	OUT				
THURSDAY	IN				
	OUT				
	IN				
	OUT				
FRIDAY	IN				
	OUT				
	IN				
	OUT				
SATURDAY	IN				
	OUT				
	IN				
	OUT				
SUNDAY	IN			10:00	
	OUT	6 1/2		1/2 hr.	
	IN				
	OUT			5:00	

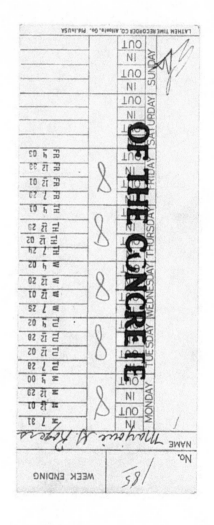

Acknowledgements:

Thank you:

To Megan O'Connell of Salt & Cedar Letterpress for so graciously welcoming me into your space in the summer of 2016 - I'm grateful to have gotten a glimpse into your world. To Matthew Gavin Frank for your guidance and your copious, sprawling notes. To Rachel May and Caroline Krzakowski for the insights and feedback you brought to the project - I have such appreciation or your thoughfulness. To NMU for the generous research funding that provided critical support for the project, as well as for graciously giving me access to the letterpress hidden away on the second floor of the art building. To Ania, Sara, and Sarah whose friendships were some of the best things to come from three years of living in a barren tundra. To Christin Lee and Room Project for providing me a desk to work at every Thursday morning during a very desolate winter, as well as a much needed sense of community. To my parents John and Marilyn for years and years (and years) of support. And to Detroit - for being so unknowable and confounding and entrancing all at once.

*A note on the timecard images throughout the book - these timecards were gathered by the art collective, YOURSELF, in the winter of 2015 at a defunct factory in the Milwaukee Junction neighborhood of Detroit (the factory's origin was never determined). They were printed in thewinter of 2017 at the School of Art and Design at Northern Michigan University.

The Meat Grinder on Riopelle Street. Quarter After Eight, Spring 2019.

On Blight (and curcubit downey mildew). saltfront: studies in human habit(at), Fall 2018.

CPSIA information can be obtained
at www.ICGtesting.com
Printed in the USA
BVHW080946160822
644713BV00007B/309